Luna Bella Publishing

Made in the USA
Columbia, SC
15 December 2022

74074099R00057